THE Forgiveness OF JESUS

PARTICIPANT'S GUIDE

The Deeper Connections Series

The Miracles of Jesus

The Last Days of Jesus

The Forgiveness of Jesus

The Life of Jesus

Deeper CONNECTIONS

THE Forgiveness OF JESUS

PARTICIPANT'S GUIDE

Six In-depth Studies Connecting the Bible to Life

Matt Williams
General Editor

ROSE
PUBLISHING

Deeper Connections:
The Forgiveness of Jesus Participant's Guide
© 2009, 2017 Matt Williams

Published by Rose Publishing
An imprint of Tyndale House Ministries
Carol Stream, Illinois
www.hendricksonrose.com

ISBN 978-162862-441-0

Cover design: Tammy Johnson
Interior Design: Mark Sheeres

Printed in the United States of America
020622VP

Contents

We all know Christians who are bored with Bible study — not because the Bible is boring, but because they haven't been introduced to its meaning in its first-century context and how that is significant for our lives today. When we begin to understand some of these "deeper connections" — both to the first century and to the twenty-first century — our lives are transformed.

The idea for the Deeper Connections series grew out of a concern that far too many Bible studies lack depth and solid biblical application. We wanted a Bible study series that was written and taught by biblical experts who could also communicate that material in a *clear, practical, understandable* manner. The Deeper Connections teachers have one foot in the historical, biblical text and the other in the modern world; they not only have written numerous books, they have many years of pastoral experience. When they teach in the local church, they often hear comments such as, "Wow, I've never heard it explained that way before." Unfortunately, that's because, until recently, Bible professors usually spent most of their time writing books for other professors, or occasionally for pastors, and the layperson in the church had little access to this biblical knowledge. Deeper Connections seeks to remedy this by bringing the best in biblical scholarship directly to small groups and Sunday school classes through the popular medium of DVD.

Don't be scared by the word "deeper." Deeper does not mean that these studies are hard to understand. It simply means that we are attempting to get at the true meaning of the biblical text, which involves investigating the historical, religious, and social background of first-century Jewish culture and their Greek and Roman neighbors. If we fail to study and understand this background, then we also fail to understand the deeper and true meaning of the Bible.

After making deeper connections to the biblical texts, the teachers then apply that text to life in the twenty-first century. This is where a deeper look into the text really pays off. Life-application in the church today has sometimes been a bit shallow and many times unrelated to the biblical passage itself. In this series, the practical application derives directly out of the biblical text.

So, to borrow the alternate title of *The Hobbit*, J. R. R. Tolkien's bestselling classic, we invite you to join us on an adventure to "there and back again"! Your life won't be the same as a result.

About the Video Teachers

Dr. Darrell Bock is research professor of New Testament Studies at Dallas Theological Seminary in Dallas, Texas. An editor-at-large for *Christianity Today*, he speaks and teaches on the person of Jesus both nationally and internationally. Darrell is the author of more than twenty books, including a *New York Times* nonfiction bestseller and two commentaries on the gospel of Luke.

Dr. Gary Burge is professor of New Testament at Wheaton College in Wheaton, Illinois, and a sought-after conference speaker. His experiences in Beirut, Lebanon, in the early 1970s when civil war broke out have helped him to see how valuable it is to understand the world of the Middle East in order to correctly understand the biblical world of Jesus. Gary is the author of many books, including a commentary on the gospel of John.

Dr. Scott Duvall is professor of New Testament at Ouachita Baptist University in Little Rock, Arkansas, where he has won the Outstanding Faculty Award four times. He has pastored various churches, and presently is co-pastor of Fellowship Church in Arkadelphia, Arkansas. Scott has written many books on how to interpret, preach, and apply the Bible.

Prof. Susan Hecht is instructor of New Testament at Denver Seminary in Denver, Colorado. She is currently completing a doctorate in New Testament from Trinity Evangelical Divinity School, before which she ministered on college campuses with Campus Crusade for Christ for twenty years in Colorado, Oregon, and North Carolina. Susan has written on the topic of ministry to postmoderns.

Dr. Mark Strauss is professor of New Testament at Bethel Seminary in San Diego, California. He is a frequent preacher at San Diego area churches and has served in three interim pastorates. Mark is the author of many books, including a commentary on the gospel of Luke and *Four Portraits, One Jesus: An Introduction to Jesus and the Gospels.*

Dr. Matt Williams is associate professor of New Testament at Talbot School of Theology, Biola University, La Mirada, California. A former missionary to Spain, Matt preaches and teaches in churches throughout the United States and Spain. He is general editor of *Biblioteca Teológica Vida, Colección Teológica Contemporánea*, and *What the New Testament Authors Really Cared About*, and is the author of two books on the Gospels.

Host **Margaret Feinberg** (www.margaretfeinberg.com) is a popular speaker at churches and leading conferences such as Fusion, Catalyst, and National Pastors Convention. Named one of the "Thirty Emerging Voices" of Christian leaders under age forty by *Charisma* magazine, she has written more than 700 articles and a dozen books, including *The Organic God* and *The Sacred Echo*. She lives in Colorado.

The Forgiving Father

The Parable of the Prodigal Son
(Luke 15:1–2, 11–24)

Dr. Matt Williams

But while he was still a long way off, his father saw him and was filled with compassion for him; he ran to his son, threw his arms around him and kissed him.

Luke 15:20

There are no grudges; the past pain has been washed away in the waves of joy at the son's return.

Darrell Bock

11

INTRODUCTION

Video Opener from Israel

Scripture Reading: Luke 15:1–2, 11–24, followed by a prayer that God will open your heart as you study his Word

Location of Passage: Probably in Galilee, on the way to Jerusalem (Luke 9:51)

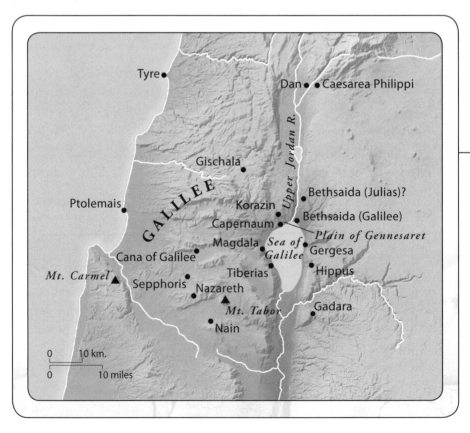

MAKING DEEPER CONNECTIONS TO THE BIBLE

The son has no idea what is going to happen to him when he returns home.

Video Teaching #1 Notes

NOTE: In each session of this participant's guide, the "Video Teaching Notes" sections give an outline of the video teaching, with additional quotes and biblical passages. Educators have proved that the teacher's main points will be remembered better if you follow along in the guide and see the main teaching points, and even better if you jot down notes in the spaces provided.

Location of Video Teaching: Box Canyon, Wickenburg, Arizona

The son returns to his father

First-century Middle Eastern glasses

Tax collectors

> Now the tax collectors and "sinners" were all gathering around to hear him.
>
> Luke 15:1

Jesus ate with sinners

DID YOU KNOW?

To eat with another person in the Mideast is a sacramental act signifying acceptance on a very deep level.

Kenneth Bailey

> But the Pharisees and the teachers of the law muttered, "This man welcomes sinners and eats with them."
>
> Luke 15:2

"Give me my share of the estate" (Luke 15:12)

The father gives the son his money

The son went to a distant land

> Not long after that, the younger son got together all he had, set off for a distant country ...
>
> Luke 15:13a

Squandered his wealth

> ... and there squandered his wealth in wild living. After he had spent everything, there was a severe famine in that whole country, and he began to be in need.
>
> Luke 15:13b–14

Feeding pigs

> So he went and hired himself out to a citizen of that country, who sent him to his fields to feed pigs. He *longed* to fill his stomach with the pods that the pigs were eating, but no one gave him anything.
>
> Luke 15:15–16

The son comes to his senses (Luke 15:17)

The plan

> When he came to his senses, he said, "How many of my father's hired men have food to spare, and here I am starving to death! I will set out and go back to my father and say to him: Father, I have sinned against heaven and against you. I am no longer worthy to be called your son; make me like one of your hired men." So he got up and went to his father.
>
> Luke 15:17–20

Compassion

> But while he was still a long way off, his father saw him and was filled with compassion for him.
>
> Luke 15:20

The father runs

DID YOU KNOW?

The word *run* in Greek is the technical term used for the footraces in the stadium. "His father saw him and had compassion and *raced*."

Kenneth Bailey

Why did the father run?

If a Jewish boy lost the family inheritance among the Gentiles and dared to return home, the community would break a large pot in front of him and cry out "so-and-so is cut off from his people."

Kenneth Bailey

The father hugs and kisses the son

The son repents

The son said to him, "Father, I have sinned against heaven and against you. I am no longer worthy to be called your son."

Luke 15:21

Robe

Ring

Shoes

His tattered garments are to be covered with the best robe; the feet that have made the long journey are to be outfitted; his hand that has become a laborer's hand is to be decorated with a fine dress ring.

John Nolland

Fatted calf

> "Bring the fattened calf and kill it. Let's have a feast and celebrate. For this son of mine was dead and is alive again; he was lost and is found." So they began to celebrate.
>
> Luke 15:23–24

VIDEO DISCUSSION #1: MAKING DEEPER CONNECTIONS TO THE BIBLE

NOTE: In each session of the participant's guide, "Video Discussion #1" mainly focuses on understanding the *meaning of the biblical text* in all its depth and fullness. Please see the leader's guide for the amount of time your group should discuss the following questions before moving on to Video Teaching #2, Connecting the Bible to Life.

1. Looking back at the Bible passage and your video teaching notes, what did you learn that you did not know previously? Consider specifically:

   • The role of tax collectors

   • The significance of the younger son asking for his inheritance

- The use of the word "compassion" in the Gospels

- What the community would have done when the son returned home

2. Given what you have just learned, why do you think the father gave his son his inheritance? Did it make sense to do so in their culture? Imagine that your child asked you for his/her inheritance; would you give it to him/her?

3. Explain the significance in this story of the father running to his son. Why do you think he did that? Imagine that you were the son in the story, and you saw your father running toward you; what would you have thought was going to happen next?

4. On good days, who is God to you? Good or bad? Forgiving or condemning? Loving or withholding? On bad days, does your answer change? Spend a few moments thanking God that his loving and forgiving character never changes.

CONNECTING THE BIBLE TO LIFE

The Father will forgive us as many times as he needs to.

Video Teaching #2 Notes

The Father forgives

> God does not wait passively for sinners to come to him, but actively seeks them out.
>
> Leon Morris

Physical benefits of forgiveness

The Father takes away our shame

> Sing, O Daughter of Zion; shout aloud, O Israel! Be glad and rejoice with all your heart, O Daughter of Jerusalem! The LORD has taken away your punishment, he has turned back your enemy. The LORD, the King of Israel, is with you; never again will you fear any harm. On that day they will say to Jerusalem, "Do not fear, O Zion; do not let your hands hang limp. The LORD your God is with you, he is mighty to save. He will take great delight in you, he will quiet you with his love, he will rejoice over you with singing."
>
> Zephaniah 3:14–17

The Father celebrates when we return

A community that accepts

> The goal of the church is not to shoot its wounded to death, but to restore them.
>
> Darrell Bock

We are the hands of the Father, offering forgiveness

A Father who forgives!

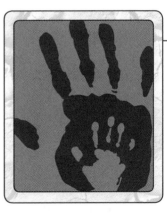

> The son is received back into the family with full honor and privileges, as if nothing has happened.
>
> Darrell Bock

Don't be afraid to
return to the Father

VIDEO DISCUSSION #2: CONNECTING THE BIBLE TO LIFE

NOTE: While "Video Discussion #1" mainly focused on the meaning of the biblical text, "Video Discussion #2" in each session mainly focuses on *applying* the biblical text to our lives today. Please see the leader's guide for the amount of time your group should discuss the following questions.

1. Have you ever been forgiven by someone after doing something bad? How did it make you feel to have been forgiven? How does it make you feel to be forgiven by your heavenly Father?

2. Spend time in prayer, meditating on whether or not you have fully received God's forgiveness for your sins, and whether or not you have fully given over all of your shame to him. If anything comes to mind as you pray: ask for God's forgiveness, ask him to take all of your shame, and then rejoice that he has done just that.

3. Matt Williams talked about the need for the Christian community today to accept people instead of judging them. This does not mean that we just accept any behavior as okay, because even in this parable, the son repents of his sins. How would you rate your Christian community's job of extending God's forgiveness to those who are seeking to grow in holiness? What could the church — yours included — do to better extend forgiveness?

4. We should never fear "going home" to our heavenly Father, no matter what we have done, or how many times we have done it. (Remember, Jesus taught his followers to forgive seventy-times-seven times, a figurative way of saying "without limit.") When you sin, how do you view God: waiting to welcome and forgive you, or waiting to scold you? What can we do to change a faulty perspective?

MAKING DEEPER CONNECTIONS IN YOUR OWN LIFE

Personal reflection studies to do on your own.

Day One

1. Read Matthew 1:18–21. What is the meaning of Jesus' name?

2. The way that we were raised affects the way that we view ourselves. If we had parents who were unloving or guilt-inducing, it will be harder to see God as loving and guilt-removing. Who is God to you? How does your "stuff" affect your view of God?

3. Did you know that when the younger son asked for his inheritance that he was wishing that his father were dead? What difference does that detail make to the story? What does it show us about God (the Father)?

Day Two

1. Read Matthew 11:25–30.

2. Have you ever done something wrong, but were too embarrassed or ashamed to admit it to anyone? How did/does that make you feel? Did it affect how you viewed yourself and/ or others? Were you afraid to approach God ... or did it move you toward him more quickly? Remember, God already knows about your sin; you can't hide it from him.

3. Let the Father run to you today. Give all of your concerns, your guilt, your shame, your sin to him — and allow him to take them all away. Consider asking a close friend to pray with you and for you.

Day Three

1. Read Matthew 9:9–13.

2. Who do you think are the hated groups (like tax collectors) today? How do the Christians in your community treat these groups? How do you treat them?

3. How is it possible to "love the sinner, but hate the sin"? Have you found the balance in being around sinners so that the love of God can infect them, or do you mostly stay away from sinners because their sin infects or tempts you? How do you think Jesus was able to be around sinners without being tempted?

Day Four

1. Read Matthew 9:1–2.

2. Look up each use of the word "compassion" in the following verses: Matthew 9:36; 14:14; 15:32; 20:34; Mark 1:41; 6:34; 8:2; Luke 15:20. Do you think that you have that kind of compassion in your life?

3. When the Gospels tell us that God or Jesus is compassionate, an action is almost always linked with it. Look back once more at the verses from question two, and ask yourself if *your* compassion leads you to action. Does it lead to the same kinds of actions that Jesus did, or are they different?

Day Five

1. Read Luke 15:1–2, 11–24 one more time.

2. Pray through the entire passage verse by verse, allowing the deeper meaning that you have discovered to lead you as you pray. Ask the Spirit to continue to remind you of what you have learned and to help you apply these truths to your life. Jot down any further applications that come to mind as you pray.

3. Turn back to the discussion questions from the video teaching (Video Discussion #1, #2). If there are questions that your group did not have time to discuss or questions that you might like to think more about, use this time to review and reflect further.

Two Aspects of Healing

Jesus Forgives the Paralytic (Mark 2:1–12)

Prof. Susan Hecht

"But that you may know that the Son of Man has authority on earth to forgive sins. . . ." He said to the paralytic, "I tell you, get up, take your mat and go home."

Mark 2:10 – 11

God is for healing.

David Garland

INTRODUCTION

Video Opener from Israel

Scripture Reading: Mark 2:1–12, followed by a prayer that God will open your heart as you study his Word

Location of Passage: Capernaum

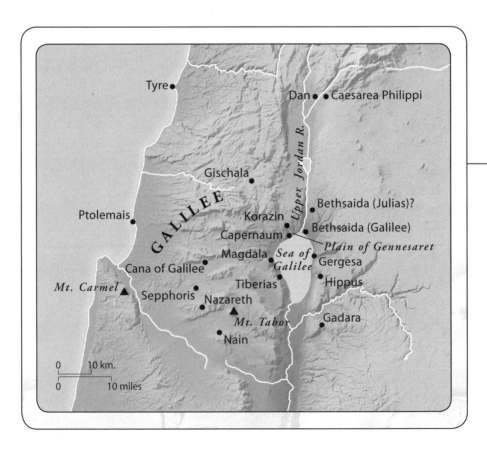

MAKING DEEPER CONNECTIONS TO THE BIBLE

Jesus' miracles reveal that he truly can and does forgive sins. In him there is real hope for healing and wholeness on every level of our existence.

Video Teaching #1 Notes

Location of Video Teaching: Glen Eyrie Castle, Colorado Springs

My brother

"Paralytic": modern meaning

"Paralytic" in the New Testament

Issues of healing were important in the first century, because the ability to care for the sick was limited.

Darrell Bock

Mark 1: large crowds

Four men carry the
paralytic to Jesus

Jesus forgives the paralytic

When Jesus saw their faith, he said to the paralytic, "Son, your sins are
forgiven."

Mark 2:5

Sin and physical illness in antiquity

DID YOU KNOW?

Jewish tradition understands that all sickness is caused, directly or indirectly, by sin.

D. A. Carson

"Rabbi, who sinned, this man or his parents, that he was born blind?" "Neither this man nor his parents sinned."

John 9:2–3

Only God can forgive sins

Jewish expectation did not include forgiveness among the Messiah's functions.

R. T. France

Jesus is fulfilling Old Testament prophecies

Then will the eyes of the blind be opened and the ears of the deaf unstopped. Then will the lame leap like a deer, and the mute tongue shout for joy.

Isaiah 35:5–6

The Pharisees accuse Jesus of blasphemy

Blasphemy was a capital offense (Lev. 24:10–16), and it will be on this charge that Jesus is eventually condemned—so the matter is serious.

R. T. France

Jesus' response to the Pharisees

Why are you thinking these things? Which is easier: to say to the paralytic, "Your sins are forgiven," or to say, "Get up, take your mat and walk"?

Mark 2:8–9

Jesus' claim to forgive sins

"But that you may know that the Son of Man has authority on earth to forgive sins...." He said to the paralytic, "I tell you, get up, take your mat and go home."

Mark 2:10–11

"Son of Man"

> In my vision at night I looked, and there before me was one like a son of man, coming with the clouds of heaven. He approached the Ancient of Days and was led into his presence. He was given authority, glory and sovereign power; all peoples, nations and men of every language worshiped him. His dominion is an everlasting dominion that will not pass away, and his kingdom is one that will never be destroyed.
>
> Daniel 7:13–14

Jesus came to bring the kingdom of God

> No one living in Zion will say, "I am ill"; and the sins of those who dwell there will be forgiven.
>
> Isaiah 33:24

Jesus is more than the Messiah; he is God

The miracles of healing confirm Jesus' divine origin and power.

David Garland

The paralytic is healed and the crowd praises God

He got up, took his mat and walked out in full view of them all. This amazed everyone and they praised God, saying, "We have never seen anything like this!"

Mark 2:12

VIDEO DISCUSSION #1: MAKING DEEPER CONNECTIONS TO THE BIBLE

1. Looking back at the Bible passage and your video teaching notes, what did you learn that you did not know previously? Consider specifically:

   • The meaning of the term "paralytic" in the New Testament

   • The relationship between sin and physical illness in first-century Judaism

   • Jesus' ability to forgive sins as a divine activity

2. How did Jesus "see" the paralytic's faith? Isn't faith something in one's heart — simply a belief? If Jesus were here today, could he "see" your faith in your daily activities? What would he "see"?

3. Although we have no way of knowing for sure, what do you think meant more to the man who was healed in this story: forgiveness of sins or the ability to walk? Given Jewish backgrounds in the first century, do you think he would have expected to receive both from Jesus?

4. When you come to Jesus, how often are you seeking him to meet your spiritual needs versus your physical or material needs? Do you expect him to meet both? If not, what difference would it make if you expected him to meet *all* your needs?

CONNECTING THE BIBLE TO LIFE

Jesus is the only one who can forgive me.

Video Teaching #2 Notes

Accepting forgiveness is sometimes hard

> If we confess our sins, he is faithful and just and will forgive us our sins and purify us from all unrighteousness.
>
> 1 John 1:9

Desperate to get to Jesus

Forgiveness from God affects the way I treat others

> If he sins against you seven times in a day, and seven times comes back to you and says, "I repent," forgive him.
>
> Luke 17:4

The church should extend forgiveness to others

Christians talk about hating sin and loving sinners, but the way they go about things, they might as well call it what it is. They hate the sin *and* the sinner.

Jeff, 25 years old

Bear with each other and forgive whatever grievances you may have against one another. Forgive as the Lord forgave you.

Colossians 3:13

Forgiveness was at the heart of Jesus' ministry

She will give birth to a son, and you are to give him the name Jesus, because he will save his people from their sins.

Matthew 1:21

My car: forgiving my friend

Forgive us our sins, for we also forgive everyone who sins against us.

Luke 11:4

Praising God for forgiveness

Jesus is the only one on the earth with the power and right to forgive sins.

W. D. Davies

"You're forgiven, aren't you?"

Though I struggle with feelings of guilt and shame, when I confess my sins, believing that they are forgiven in Jesus, the natural response is to praise God—Jesus releases me from all my guilt and shame—and then I can keep moving forward.

Susan Hecht

VIDEO DISCUSSION #2:
CONNECTING THE BIBLE TO LIFE

1. The paralytic and his four friends had a desperate need to go to Jesus—the friends carried the paralytic, dug through the roof, and lowered him down through the opening to Jesus. They needed to get to Jesus because they were convinced that he could help them. Do you have that same level of desperation, knowing that only Jesus can help you? Why or why not?

2. What is one area of your life about which you are convinced that only Jesus can help you? Do you go to him to help you? Either individually or as a group, spend some time right now to take that concern to Jesus in prayer, asking him to help.

3. Psychologists have only recently begun to research the effects of extending and receiving forgiveness. Initial findings show that forgiveness and reconciliation reduce sadness, anger, guilt, and shame—while increasing hope and more positive emotions. Can you think of a time when someone forgave you for doing wrong? How did that make you feel? Can you think of a time when you were not forgiven? How did that make you feel?

4. Knowing that Jesus has authority to forgive sins is a truth that each person must grapple with: do we believe it or not? For Christians, the answer is a resounding yes! Even so, many Christians struggle with the fact that although they *know* that Jesus forgives sins, they don't always *feel* forgiven. What are ways that we can *experience* the forgiveness we *know* is available to us? What have you found that has helped you?

MAKING DEEPER CONNECTIONS IN YOUR OWN LIFE

Personal reflection studies to do on your own.

Day One

1. Read Matthew 9:1–8. Note any similarities to and differences from Mark 2:1–10.

2. If Jesus has the authority to forgive sins, then what would it look like for you to live moment by moment as if you believed it? To put that question into clearer focus, what would your life look like if you did *not* believe that Jesus has authority to forgive sins—*your* sins?

3. Pray about your life. Ask the Lord to show you any areas that still need to be forgiven. If you cannot think of any, thank God for his forgiveness and the difference it has made. If you know that you are forgiven, but still do not fully *feel* God's forgiveness, ask him to confirm his love, compassion, and forgiveness for *you*. Sometimes it helps to experience forgiveness in the context of the relationships that God has brought into our lives. Sometimes emotional scars need healing in order for us to experience forgiveness — and that may mean working through those scars with a pastor, counselor/therapist, or mature Christian who can help us along in the process.

Day Two

1. Read Luke 5:18–26. Note any similarities to and differences from Mark 2:1–10.

2. As Susan Hecht mentioned, those of us who are forgiven also have the privilege and responsibility to forgive those who have wronged us. Take some time in prayer to ask the Lord to bring to mind any person whom you have not forgiven. Then decide on action steps you could take to begin the process of forgiveness and reconciliation.

3. In the passage we have studied, the four friends brought their paralytic friend to Jesus to receive help. Certainly there are many people in your community who do not even understand their need for help and forgiveness. Ask the Lord to show you how you could bring those people face-to-face with Jesus, with the hope that they will see their need for forgiveness. What specific actions could you take to help those in your community?

Day Three

1. Read Luke 7:16 and Matthew 15:31.

2. Mark 2:12 says, "This [Jesus' healing and forgiveness of the paralytic] amazed everyone and they praised God, saying, 'We have never seen anything like this!'" When was the last time that you were "amazed" at what Jesus has done in your life or in the life of someone else? Do you pray that God would do amazing things in your life and the lives of others? Why or why not?

3. When was the last time that you "praised God" for the amazing things that he has done in your life and in the lives of others? Take time right now to list some of those amazing things, and then praise him for them.

Day Four

1. Read Revelation 21:1–4.

2. The story of the paralytic illustrates that not only can Jesus forgive sins, but he also can physically heal. Healing, of course, comes in a variety of forms: physical, spiritual, mental, social, etc. What type of healing do you think people in your church most need to experience? Your family? Your community? What about your own needs for healing from Jesus?

3. We know that when the kingdom of God comes in its fullness, physical ailments will cease. David Garland says, "God is for healing and therefore can work through medicine and surgery as much as faith and prayer" (*Mark*, NIVAC, 100). Do you think that Jesus is still interested in healing people in every way today, in the twenty-first century, or was that just for the early church? Do you emphasize all forms of healing when you minister to people?

Day Five

1. Read Mark 2:1–12 one more time.

2. Pray through the entire passage verse by verse, allowing the deeper meaning that you have discovered to lead you as you pray. Ask the Spirit to continue to remind you of what you have learned and to help you apply these truths to your life. Jot down any further applications that come to mind as you pray.

3. Turn back to the discussion questions from the video teaching (Video Discussion #1, #2). If there are questions that your group did not have time to discuss or questions that you might like to think more about, use this time to review and reflect further.

Spiritual Sight

Jesus Heals a
Man Born Blind
(John 9:1 – 15, 34 – 41)

Dr. Gary Burge

One thing I do know. I was blind
but now I see!

John 9:25

More than a mere miracle, this
sign represents a highly symbolic
display of Jesus' ability to cure
spiritual blindness.

Andreas Köstenberger

INTRODUCTION

Video Opener from Israel

Jewish temple (reconstruction)

Scripture Reading: John 9:1 – 15, 34 – 41, followed by a prayer that God will open your heart as you study his Word

Location of Passage: Near the temple in Jerusalem

MAKING DEEPER CONNECTIONS TO THE BIBLE

The healing of a blind man who lives in darkness is the perfect symbol of what Jesus came to do.

Video Teaching #1 Notes

Location of Video Teaching: Millennium Park, Chicago

Blindness of heart and eyes are similar

Blindness in the ancient world

Jesus was a great healer

DID YOU KNOW?

Blindness was one of the grimmest maladies in the ancient world and was considered to be only a little less serious than being dead.

Michael Wilkins

Great crowds came to him, bringing the lame, the blind, the crippled, the mute and many others, and laid them at his feet; and he healed them.

Matthew 15:30

In Judaism, blindness was a punishment for sin

The LORD will afflict you with madness, *blindness* and confusion of mind. At midday you will grope about like a *blind man* in the dark.

Deuteronomy 28:28–29

There is no death without sin, and there is no suffering with iniquity.

Rabbi Ammi (c. AD 300)

Jesus sees blindness as an opportunity to show compassion

The blind man in John 9

What else could a blind man do in the ancient world than beg?

Leon Morris

The disciples: "Who sinned, this man or his parents?" (John 9:2)

Jesus rejects the Jewish understanding of sin and blindness

"Neither this man nor his parents sinned," said Jesus, "but this happened so that the work of God might be displayed in his life."

John 9:3

"Neither this man nor his parents sinned," said Jesus. [Period.] But *so that* the work of God might be displayed in his life, I must do the work of him who sent me while it is still day.

Gary Burge

Jesus heals the blind man

DID YOU KNOW?

In antiquity spittle was thought to have medicinal power ... even magical power.

Gary Burge

Pool of Siloam ("Sent")

> "My food," said Jesus, "is to do the will of him who sent me and to finish his work."
>
> John 4:34

The neighbors' reaction

The Pharisees' reaction

DID YOU KNOW?

Kneading dough (and, by analogy, mixing clay and saliva) was among the thirty-nine classes of work forbidden on the day of Sabbath.

Mishnah *Sabbath* 7:2

The parents of the blind man

Sinners ...

> A second time they summoned the man who had been blind. "Give glory to God," they said. "We know this man [Jesus] is a sinner." He replied, "Whether he is a sinner or not, I don't know. One thing I do know. I was blind but now I see!"
>
> John 9:24–25

Without eyes of faith, the Pharisees cannot see that God is doing something unique through Jesus.

Michael Wilkins

The blind man lectures the Pharisees

> [The man answered,] "Nobody has ever heard of opening the eyes of a man born blind. If this man were not from God, he could do nothing."
>
> John 9:32–33

The end of the debate with the Pharisees

> To this they replied, "You were steeped in sin at birth; how dare you lecture us!" And they threw him out.
>
> John 9:34

Jesus meets the blind man again

Concluding remarks

> While I am in the world, I am the light of the world.
>
> John 9:5

Light has triumphed over darkness both in the blind man's eyes and in his heart.

Gary Burge

VIDEO DISCUSSION #1: MAKING DEEPER CONNECTIONS TO THE BIBLE

1. Looking back at the Bible passage and your video teaching notes, what did you learn that you did not know previously? Consider specifically:

   • The difficulty of blindness in the first century

   • The relationship of blindness and sin in Judaism

   • The reaction of the Pharisees to the healing

2. Imagine the personal impact of this miracle on the man. Jesus didn't just give him back his eyesight, he returned his life to him. As Jesus said, "The thief comes only to steal and kill and destroy; I have come that they may have life, and have it to the *full*" (John 10:10). Specifically, how do you think the man's life changed after he gained his sight? Think spiritually, but also socially, religiously, physically, even his sudden ability to earn a living. Do you think most Christians today view salvation as being healed in every area of life, or is it just forgiveness of sins?

3. Why do you think the Jewish leaders had such a difficult time accepting the blind man's healing? In the minds of these leaders, what had Jesus done wrong? If you had been there and witnessed the healing, do you think you would have agreed with the Jewish leaders in their assessment of Jesus? Why or why not?

4. John implies that there is another sort of darkness in human life that is as severe as blindness. It might be called "darkness of soul." At the end of the story, Jesus picks up the subject of sin and applies it to the Jewish leaders. In what sense are they blind? What is the relation between blindness and sin in their lives? What about people today—is there still a relationship between spiritual blindness and sin? Do you think we can do anything about it?

CONNECTING THE BIBLE TO LIFE

For Jesus, true vision is not just a matter of the eyes.

Video Teaching #2 Notes

Jesus looks to *touch* needy people

A step deeper: blindness of heart

The hopelessness and darkness of the blind man provide us with a potent image because John describes men and women without Christ to be in a crisis no less desperate.

Gary Burge

Feast of Tabernacles

Light ceremony in the temple

At the end of the first day of the feast, three eighty-foot-high golden candlesticks were set up in the temple's Court of Women. Four golden bowls were placed on each candlestick, and four ladders rested against each. A youth of priestly descent stood at the top of each ladder, pouring oil from a ten-gallon pitcher into the bowl. The light from these candlesticks was so bright that "there was no courtyard in Jerusalem that was not lit up with the light at the ceremony."

Mishnah *Sukkah* 5:3

"I am the light of the world" (John 8:12)

The blind man encounters the Light

> Jesus heard that they had thrown him out, and when he found him, he said, "Do you believe in the Son of Man?" "Who is he, sir?" the man asked. "Tell me so that I may believe in him." Jesus said, "You have now seen him; in fact, he is the one speaking with you." Then the man said, "Lord, I believe," and he worshiped him.
>
> John 9:35–38

The Pharisees "know" many things

The blind man knows one thing

> One thing I do know. I was blind but now I see!
>
> John 9:25

Certainly countless Christians have applied the same words to their own transformation: *One thing I do know. I was blind but now I see!*

D. A. Carson

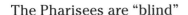

The Pharisees are "blind"

> Some Pharisees who were with him heard him say this and asked, "What? Are we blind too?" Jesus said, "If you were blind, you would not be guilty of sin; but now that you claim you can see, your guilt remains."
>
> John 9:40–41

True vision is not just a matter of the eyes

Story of Pastor Bob

Jesus is eager to heal closed eyes *and* closed hearts

Physical healing becomes a symbol of spiritual healing while physical blindness is replaced with spiritual blindness.

Gary Burge

Chicago: blindness of soul and physical blindness

Jesus touched the blind man and gave him life

The thief comes only to steal and kill and destroy; I have come that they may have life, and have it to the full.

John 10:10

VIDEO DISCUSSION #2: CONNECTING THE BIBLE TO LIFE

1. The blind man probably sat at a roadside and begged. No employment, no prospects of marriage, no social honor. His future was bleak and he knew it. This hopelessness and darkness provide us with a potent image because John describes men and women without Christ to be in a crisis no less desperate. Do you think of people without Jesus, even those who seem to have it all together, as "blind"?

2. The healing of the blind man is located in John's account of Jesus attending the Jewish Feast of Tabernacles (chs. 7–9). As Gary Burge mentioned, the important symbolism of this feast relates directly to the meaning of the passage. Jesus has already said that he is the light of the world (8:12); now he is delivering that light to a blind man. How is Jesus the "light of the world" in your life? How is he the "light of the world" to those in your family, neighborhood, community? How could *you* be a conduit of his light to these people?

3. In this story, the blind man, his neighbors, and the Pharisees all saw the same evidence—a man blind from birth was now able to see. Now we must ask ourselves: Will I, like the blind man, believe that Jesus is the light of the world and worship him no matter the cost? Or, like the Jewish leaders, will I ask antagonistic questions? Which camp do you normally fall into? The blind man was thrown out of the synagogue for following Jesus. What has it "cost you" to worship Jesus?

4. The Jewish leaders were deeply religious, had a high view of Scripture, believed in the afterlife, regularly attended worship, and apparently were zealous and passionate for God. Sound familiar? Therefore we must ask: Can "darkness of soul" ever spread in the church? And if so, what does it look like?

MAKING DEEPER CONNECTIONS IN YOUR OWN LIFE

Personal reflection studies to do on your own.

Day One

1. Read John 10:9–15.

2. Though we may wear masks to keep up appearances, we are all depraved and in need of a Savior. As we see the sins of others revealed, the last thing on our minds should be the Pharisaic attitude of condemnation. Instead, we should remember that we *all* share in this brokenness. Think about how you react when you see the weaknesses of others. Do you respond more like the Pharisees or more like Jesus?

3. The blind man was certainly excluded from his community, who thought that he was a sinner being punished by God with blindness. You and I probably do not suffer from blindness or face the daily shame that the blind man did. We probably are not excluded from our community or spend the day begging for food. Yet, even though we do not face all the same hardships, do we still see our desperate need for Jesus? Do we understand that only he can address every one of our needs?

Day Two

1. Read 1 John 1:9.

2. Jesus asked the blind man, "Do you believe in the Son of Man?" (John 9:35). How would you answer? Do you believe in Jesus? Not the superficial type of belief that we often see in Christianity, but belief that fully grasps on to Jesus with your whole life—accepting whatever he has for you, willing to do anything that he asks?

3. The account in John ends with the man worshiping Jesus. He worships Jesus because Jesus has healed him—not just of his physical blindness, but his spiritual blindness—and has restored him to his community. As you pray today, worship the God who has restored you from a broken relationship with him to "full life." List below all the ways that God has blessed you and "healed" you.

Day Three

1. Read John 3:16–21.

2. Jesus brings light both to the blind man and the Pharisees. Light reveals whatever is within a person, good or bad. This means that the light of Christ both brings life and judgment. When the light of Jesus shines on you and illumines the weak areas of your life, how do you respond? Do you want to stay in the light so that Jesus can help you, or do you run away?

3. The blind man's response—"Lord, I believe"—should echo in the life of every Christian. Is not every minute of our time spent saying either yes or no to the Lord? As we live our lives in submission to him, far be it from us to claim that by taking control of our own lives we can gain something better. In fact, we often discover that the more we make decisions for ourselves, the greater our trouble. True fullness is found in the loving arms of Jesus Christ. Meditate on the different areas of your life. Have you said, "Yes, Lord, I believe" in every area—family, friends, possessions, time, job, hobbies, etc.?

Day Four

1. Read John 14:11–14.

2. Go online to study the background of the Feast of Tabernacles and its emphasis on light. The Feast of Tabernacles was celebrated, principally, to thank God for a good harvest of wine, fruit, olives, and secondarily, to remember his care for the Israelites in the desert following the exodus from Egypt. The feast also looked forward, with hope, to a new exodus from slavery to pagan rulers in Jesus' day. Into this context Jesus brings freedom to the blind. Enjoy the discovery of learning today. Jot any notes of insight below.

3. Just as in the first century, Jesus' messianic mission continues to shine as a light to a dark, depraved world. One day he will come again in glory to rescue us from the dominion of Satan and to judge the living and the dead. Do you grow weary living in this world? Do you remember your mission? Do you remember that Jesus will return, and what we do here on earth makes an eternal difference for him? Think about whether or not your life is making an eternal difference for Jesus.

Day Five

1. Read John 9:1–15, 34–41 one more time.

2. Pray through the entire passage verse by verse, allowing the deeper meaning that you have discovered to lead you as you pray. Ask the Spirit to continue to remind you of what you have learned and to help you apply these truths to your life. Jot down any further applications that come to mind as you pray.

3. Turn back to the discussion questions from the video teaching (Video Discussion #1, #2). If there are questions that your group did not have time to discuss or questions that you might like to think more about, use this time to review and reflect further.

Hope for Sinners

Jesus' Dinner Invitation (Matthew 9:9–13)

Dr. Scott Duvall

While Jesus was having dinner at Matthew's house, many tax collectors and "sinners" came and ate with him and his disciples.

Matthew 9:10

Jesus shows no fear that he will be tainted by the impurity of sinners. On the contrary, he will infect them with the grace of God.

David Garland

INTRODUCTION

Video Opener from Israel

Scripture Reading: Matthew 9:9–13, followed by a prayer that God will open your heart as you study his Word

Location of Passage: Near Capernaum

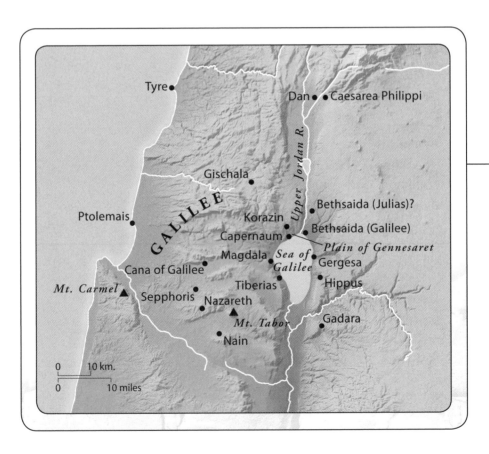

MAKING DEEPER CONNECTIONS TO THE BIBLE

Jesus seeks out sinners in order to overwhelm them with God's love and watch them change from the inside out.

Video Teaching #1 Notes

Location of Video Teaching: High school cafeteria, Little Rock, Arkansas

Cliques in our day

Cliques in Jesus' day

Silver coin depicts Tiberius, the Roman emperor during Jesus' ministry

Jesus calls Matthew

As Jesus went on from there, he saw a man named Matthew sitting at the tax collector's booth. "Follow me," he told him, and Matthew got up and followed him.

Matthew 9:9

Matthew

Tax collectors

Levi's literacy opened up a quite different career path than the one his ancestors envisioned.

David Garland

Tax collectors were dishonest

Matthew's call to be a disciple

Party

Jesus eats with sinners

> While Jesus was having dinner at Matthew's house, many tax collectors and "sinners" came and ate with him and his disciples.
>
> Matthew 9:10

Matthew was an agent of the hated Herod; this made him as much an outcast from orthodox Jewish society as a leper [would have been].

R. Allen Cole

The Pharisees are offended by Jesus

> When the Pharisees saw this, they asked his disciples, "Why does your teacher eat with tax collectors and 'sinners'?"
>
> Matthew 9:11

[If] tax collectors ... entered the house—the house [was considered] unclean ... unclean is the place trodden by the feet of thieves. What do they render unclean? The foods, the liquids, and clay utensils. If there is a Gentile with them, everything is unclean.

Mishnah *Tohorot* 7:6

Pharisees: quarantine approach

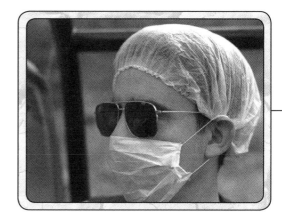

Jesus: transformation approach

DID YOU KNOW?

To eat with sinners meant to refrain from condemning them.

Leon Morris

Now the tax collectors and "sinners" were all gathering around to hear him.

Luke 15:1

Jesus answers the Pharisees

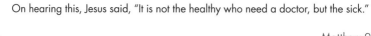
On hearing this, Jesus said, "It is not the healthy who need a doctor, but the sick."

Matthew 9:12

Pharisees: "sick" people

Jesus' definition of "sick/
sinner"

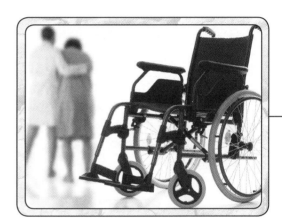

But go and learn what this means: "I desire mercy, not sacrifice." For I have not come to call the righteous, but sinners.

Matthew 9:13

Jesus calls sinners

VIDEO DISCUSSION #1: MAKING DEEPER CONNECTIONS TO THE BIBLE

1. How was Jesus running a risk by calling Matthew to be an apostle? Why do you think he took a chance on Matthew?

2. Imagine that you were sitting at the banquet among Matthew, his tax collector and "sinner" friends, and Jesus. What do you think would have been the topic(s) of conversation? Have you ever had a get-together that included both Christians and non-Christians? Did conversations occur that were about God or the gospel?

3. How would you describe in your own words the two approaches to holiness — Jesus' transformation approach versus the Pharisees' quarantine approach? Which approach is normally used in your church? Which do you use?

4. Do we understand the degree to which we can influence family, friends, neighbors, and community if we simply take the time to partake in a meal with them? Consider especially the opportunity many of us have during lunch at work. Have you ever tried this? What were the results? How could we improve these opportunities?

CONNECTING THE BIBLE TO LIFE

Because Jesus loves sinners, he calls us to develop relationships with them and to bring them to him, the Great Physician, for forgiveness and healing.

Video Teaching #2 Notes

Everyone is *spiritually* sick

Moralism

Extending hope to all outcasts
and sinners

> ## DID YOU KNOW?
>
> The term "sinners" desig-
> nated those who lived an
> immoral lifestyle (murderers,
> robbers, adulterers, a more
> criminal element).
>
> Robert Guelich

Interacting with tax collectors
and sinners

Caution

> Jesus' goal in reaching out to the sick/sinner is to bring about
> healing and transformation in their lives, not to gather them together
> for a fun time.
>
> David Garland

Compassionate
relationships

Following Jesus' example today

> Jesus reaches out to sinners because he sees the potential for their being renewed through God's grace. Jesus knows such change does not happen when those who seek sinners isolate themselves. His mission is to regain sinners by going to them.
>
> Darrell Bock

VIDEO DISCUSSION #2: CONNECTING THE BIBLE TO LIFE

1. Why are Christians often slow to follow Jesus' example and associate with sinners and other outcasts? Why is it so uncomfortable to get outside our own circles? What are some small steps we can take to follow Jesus' example in this area?

2. Jesus viewed Matthew more for what he could become rather than who he had been. Though we need to be realistic about people's sinful situation and the difficulty of change, Jesus was optimistic about God's power of forgiveness to transform a human life. Are you? Do you look at a "sinner" and see Jesus' potential to totally transform them? Why or why not?

3. The danger of sin and worldliness is real (see 1 John 2:15–17). What can we learn from Jesus about befriending sinners without embracing or endorsing their sinful ways?

4. Jesus was such a good friend that Matthew was unashamed to introduce him to tax collectors and sinners. Matthew must have known that Jesus' character would not be offensive to them. Are non-Christians or new Christians inviting you to meet their friends? How might you put yourself in a place to receive such invitations?

MAKING DEEPER CONNECTIONS IN YOUR OWN LIFE

Personal reflection studies to do on your own.

Day One

1. Read Matthew 26:6–13.

2. Christians seem to have greater opportunities for evangelism within the first few years after their conversion, before they have moved on to a new circle of friends. We should encourage new believers to be intentional about sharing Christ during this important window of opportunity and discourage them from losing contact completely with people who need the Lord. How could you encourage new believers to be intentional about evangelism, without just throwing them "out there" without help?

3. Those who seek to follow Jesus in showing compassion to outcasts will probably face opposition. Sadly, opposition will sometimes come from within the believing community, perhaps even from religious leaders, or from within one's own family. How can we respond in love to those who criticize us?

Day Two

1. Read Luke 14:1–6.

2. The Pharisees failed to understand the compassion Jesus alludes to in Hosea 6:6 because they had elevated their own rituals and traditions above God's Word. They had lost sight of the balance between God's holiness and love that we see connected in this passage. In trying to maintain purity, they had veered off into isolationism. Think about your own life: without neglecting the importance of holiness, are you allowing "rules" to restrict your ability to reach out to the "sinners" of our society?

3. What do you think Jesus thought when Matthew invited him to his home, along with his tax collector friends? Do you think it was a tough decision for Jesus to accept the invitation?

Day Three

1. Read Luke 14:15–23.

2. Read Hosea 6. How does Hosea 6:6 help us understand both God's love and God's holiness and how the two character qualities relate?

3. While sharing your faith with non-believers, have you spent a lot of time trying to convince critics of the truth claims of Christianity? Have you studied enough to be able to answer their questions? Have you balanced truth with love?

Day Four

1. Read Luke 19:1–10.

2. Who are the "tax collectors and sinners" in our society? Who are the Pharisees? Are you more like the "sinners," the Pharisees, or Jesus? As you pray today, ask Jesus to conform you more and more into his image.

3. One of Bill Hybels's favorite evangelism techniques is for Christians to throw a party, inviting both Christians and nonChristians, and letting them mingle and share stories. Consider whether or not this technique might work for you, and how you might implement it.

Day Five

1. Read Matthew 9:9–13 one more time.

2. Pray through the entire passage verse by verse, allowing the deeper meaning that you have discovered to lead you as you pray. Ask the Spirit to continue to remind you of what you have learned and to help you apply these truths to your life. Jot down any further applications that come to mind as you pray.

3. Turn back to the discussion questions from the video teaching (Video Discussion #1, #2). If there are questions that your group did not have time to discuss or questions that you might like to think more about, use this time to review and reflect further.

A Second Chance

Jesus Restores Peter
(John 21:1–17)

Dr. Mark Strauss

Jesus said, "Simon son of John, do you truly love me?" He answered, "Yes, Lord, you know that I love you." Jesus said, "Take care of my sheep."

John 21:16

The miracle demonstrates that despite Peter's failings, Jesus is still on his side.

Gary Burge

89

INTRODUCTION

Video Opener from Israel

Scripture Reading: John 21:1–17, followed by a prayer that God will open your heart as you study his Word

Location of Passage: Alongside the Sea of Galilee

MAKING DEEPER CONNECTIONS TO THE BIBLE

Jesus restores Peter. It is a painful process, but Peter needs to know that his mistake is completely forgiven.

Video Teaching #1 Notes

Location of Video Teaching: Lake Pleasant, Phoenix, Arizona

Mistakes

Peter's mistake

In the garden of Gethsemane

> Then the men stepped forward, seized Jesus and arrested him. With that, one of Jesus' companions reached for his sword, drew it out and struck the servant of the high priest, cutting off his ear. "Put your sword back in its place," Jesus said to him, "for all who draw the sword will die by the sword."
>
> Matthew 26:50–52

Peter denies Jesus

> "Certainly this fellow was with him, for he is a Galilean." Peter replied, "Man, I don't know what you're talking about!" Just as he was speaking, the rooster crowed. The Lord turned and looked straight at Peter. Then Peter remembered the word the Lord had spoken to him: "Before the rooster crows today, you will disown me three times." And he went outside and wept bitterly.
>
> Luke 22:59–62

Regret

Resurrection

Doubts ...

John 21: fishing

> "I'm going out to fish," Simon Peter told them, and they said, "We'll go with you." So they went out and got into the boat, but that night they caught nothing.
>
> John 21:3

Remarkably, the disciples never catch a fish in any of the Gospels without Jesus' help.

Andreas Köstenberger

The miraculous catch

> Early in the morning, Jesus stood on the shore, but the disciples did not realize that it was Jesus. He called out to them, "Friends, haven't you any fish?" "No," they answered. He said, "Throw your net on the right side of the boat and you will find some." When they did, they were unable to haul the net in because of the large number of fish.
>
> John 21:4–6

"It is the Lord!"

> Then the disciple whom Jesus loved said to Peter, "It is the Lord!" As soon as Simon Peter heard him say, "It is the Lord," he wrapped his outer garment around him (for he had taken it off) and jumped into the water. The other disciples followed in the boat, towing the net full of fish, for they were not far from shore, about a hundred yards. When they landed, they saw a fire of burning coals there with fish on it, and some bread.
>
> John 21:7–9

Peter swam to the only one who could rewrite the terrible pictures and sounds of his recent past.

Gary Burge

Breakfast together

Jesus said to them, "Bring some of the fish you have just caught." Simon Peter climbed aboard and dragged the net ashore. It was full of large fish, 153, but even with so many the net was not torn. Jesus said to them, "Come and have breakfast."

John 21:10–12

"Simon son of John, do you truly love me more than these?" (John 21:15)

A second time

A third time

The third time he said to him, "Simon son of John, do you love me?" Peter was hurt because Jesus asked him the third time, "Do you love me?" He said, "Lord, you know all things; you know that I love you." Jesus said, "Feed my sheep."

John 21:17

"Love" or "really like"

	Jesus	Peter
First time	agapao	phileo
Second time	agapao	phileo
Third time	phileo	phileo

Agapao and *phileo* are synonyms

DID YOU KNOW?

Agapao is used with reference to human love in John 3:19 and 12:43; *phileo* is used to refer to God the Father's love for the Son in John 5:20.

Andreas Köstenberger

Jesus calls Peter to full discipleship

Jesus fully restores Peter

Church of the Primacy of Peter

VIDEO DISCUSSION #1: MAKING DEEPER CONNECTIONS TO THE BIBLE

1. Looking back at the Bible passage and your video teaching notes, what did you learn that you did not know previously? Consider specifically:

   • The seriousness of Peter's denial of Jesus

   • The meaning of "love" (*agapao, phileo*)

2. Are you surprised that Jesus fully restored Peter? After all, Peter had denied Jesus three times in Jesus' time of need. If you were Jesus, do you think that you would have restored Peter, or would you have looked for someone "better" to be the foundation of the church?

3. Given that Jesus not only forgave Peter, but fully restored him to his position of leadership among the apostles, do you think that there is anything that *you* could do that would cause Jesus to give up on you—to *not* forgive you? Have you ever felt like you had done something for which he could not forgive you? Thank the Lord that he forgives and restores, rather than condemns you.

4. What do you think is the meaning of the phrase "more than these" in John 21:15? Do you think that it was difficult for Peter to answer "Yes, Lord" to this question? What would your answer be—do you love Jesus more than family, friends, occupation, possessions? Do your daily decisions demonstrate this?

CONNECTING THE BIBLE TO LIFE

One of the great lessons we learn from this story is that God is a God of second chances.

Video Teaching #2 Notes

God of second chances

> It was cold, and the servants and officials stood around a fire they had made to keep warm. Peter also was standing with them, warming himself.... As Simon Peter stood warming himself, he was asked, "You are not one of his disciples, are you?" He denied it, saying, "I am not."
>
> John 18:18, 25

Paul

The work of the church can only go forward when we are unburdened of our destructive memories through the gracious forgiveness of God.

Gary Burge

John Mark

> Get Mark and bring him with you, because he is helpful to me in my ministry.
>
> 2 Timothy 4:11

God restores us

God calls us to feed his sheep

> Maintaining the flock of God is the key to the mission of the church.
>
> Grant Osborne

Good Shepherd

> I am the good shepherd. The good shepherd lays down his life for the sheep.
>
> John 10:11

Conflicts in churches

To be in a relationship with Christ and to love him means that we must also love the church.

Gary Burge

God calls us to give up our lives for the kingdom

"I tell you the truth, when you were younger you dressed yourself and went where you wanted; but when you are old you will stretch out your hands, and someone else will dress you and lead you where you do not want to go." Jesus said this to indicate the kind of death by which Peter would glorify God. Then he said to him, "Follow me!"

John 21:18–19

Giving others second chances

> Be kind and compassionate to one another, forgiving each other, just as in Christ God forgave you.
>
> Ephesians 4:32

VIDEO DISCUSSION #2: CONNECTING THE BIBLE TO LIFE

1. Peter, Paul, John Mark—these are major leaders in the early church. Who doesn't need a second chance! Who doesn't need the forgiveness of Jesus over and over again! Is there anything that you have done for which you still do not "feel" God's forgiveness and restoration? Forgiveness empowers us and frees us: *frees us to love and serve others.* Spend time in the Lord's presence, asking for his forgiveness to overflow in your heart and life—maybe even asking for forgiveness for specific sins, and how that can overflow into loving and serving others.

2. Those who have been forgiven and restored, like Peter, are asked to "feed my sheep." This is not just the task of the pastor! What do you think your role is as a "shepherd"? How can you "feed" or "tend" those around you? List below anything that comes to mind.

3. According to John 21:7, Peter jumped into the water to swim to Jesus, although the fishing boat was close to the shore. This is the type of devotion that Jesus loves to see! Do you have that same kind of enthusiastic devotion to "get to Jesus" in your life? Have you jumped? Why or why not?

4. These expert fishermen (remember, that was their occupation) were unable to catch any fish. And they were fishing at night, the best time to catch fish. Yet Jesus empowered them to catch 153 fish—during the day! The disciples learned once again that "apart from me you can do nothing" (John 15:5). Have you learned that lesson? How might you better rely on Jesus' power whatever you do, wherever you go?

MAKING DEEPER CONNECTIONS IN YOUR OWN LIFE

Personal reflection studies to do on your own.

Day One

1. Read Acts 26:12–18.

2. What do you think the relationship was between Jesus' empowerment of the disciples and their own work in catching the fish? How does that relate to evangelism and other ministries in which you might be involved?

3. Pray today that the Lord would empower your own ministry, whether it is being a good witness for him in school or the workplace, or in some ministry in your community or church. If you are currently not involved in a ministry, ask the Lord to help you find a place where you might be able to use your gifts to serve him.

Day Two

1. Read Acts 15:36–40 and 2 Timothy 4:11. Notice how Paul's attitude toward John Mark changed.

2. One of the discussion questions in this session talked about everyone's need to be forgiven by Jesus. Consider spending some time on your own with the Lord, asking him to lift the burden of any regrets or doubts you still carry.

3. After Jesus restored Peter, he gave him the task of helping others. Do you see that relationship in your own life? Might you lead other "sheep"? Might you disciple others to help them to grow in their relationship with the Good Shepherd? Jot down any types of service in which you could become involved.

Day Three

1. Read Psalm 51.

2. Peter wronged Jesus in a big way. In your reading for today, Psalm 51, we see David's response to God after David had sinned in a big way with Bathsheba. In both instances, and in many others in the Bible, we see that God forgives, and gives a second chance. Do you forgive those who have offended you? Do you give others second, and third, and fourth chances? Honestly think through your different relationships to determine if you harbor unforgiveness toward anyone. If so, what could you do to reconcile that relationship?

3. We know that Jesus' mission was not "to be served, but to serve, and to give his life as a ransom for many" (Mark 10:45). It is interesting to note in John 21, however, that Jesus is still serving the disciples—even after he has been resurrected. In other words, the resurrected Lord also is a servant. He is still serving you! List below the different ways that Jesus serves you and helps you.

Day Four

1. Read Psalm 118:1–9.

2. John 6:44 says, "No one can come to me unless the Father who sent me *draws* him [her]," and in 12:32, "When I am lifted up from the earth, [I] will *draw* all [people] to myself." Interestingly, that word is used again in 21:6—the disciples could not "haul" (literally, "draw") the net into the boat because there were so many fish. Do you think that the story of the great catch shows us that Jesus will "draw" all people to himself through the disciples? Why doesn't Jesus "catch" people by himself in evangelism instead of using us? What are the benefits and costs of using us instead of just doing it himself?

3. Mark Strauss says that God calls us to feed his sheep, and tells the story about the pastor who did not lead his church with love and humility, which led to conflict. Unfortunately, conflict exists far too often in our churches. What can you do to help reduce/eliminate conflict in your church and with other Christians you know?

Day Five

1. Read John 21:1–17 one more time.

2. Pray through the entire passage verse by verse, allowing the deeper meaning that you have discovered to lead you as you pray. Ask the Spirit to continue to remind you of what you have learned and to help you apply these truths to your life. Jot down any further applications that come to mind as you pray.

3. Turn back to the discussion questions from the video teaching (Video Discussion #1, #2). If there are questions that your group did not have time to discuss or questions that you might like to think more about, use this time to review and reflect further.

Released to Forgive

Jesus Heals a Crippled Woman on the Sabbath (Luke 13:10–17)

Dr. Darrell Bock

Then should not this woman, a daughter of Abraham, whom Satan has kept bound for eighteen long years, be set free on the Sabbath day from what bound her?

Luke 13:16

God's compassion is always available, but sometimes people are more concerned with other things than with helping others.

Darrell Bock

INTRODUCTION
Video Opener from Israel

Scripture Reading: Luke 13:10–17, followed by a prayer that God will open your heart as you study his Word

Location of Passage: Jewish synagogue, location unknown

MAKING DEEPER CONNECTIONS TO THE BIBLE

Normally, healing is a good thing, but Jesus faces opposition to this healing.

Video Teaching #1 Notes

Location of Video Teaching: Dallas Holocaust Museum

Holocaust, ten Boom family

> For a long moment we grasped each other's hands, the former guard and the former prisoner. I had never known God's love so intensely as I did then.
>
> Corrie ten Boom

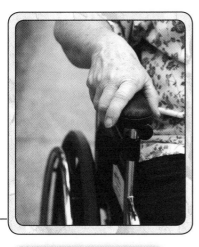

Sabbath healing

Sabbath rest conflict

DID YOU KNOW?

The rabbis debated whether it was justified to offer medical help to someone on the Sabbath.

Mark Strauss

On a Sabbath Jesus was teaching in one of the synagogues.

Luke 13:10

Jesus heals a crippled woman on the Sabbath

A woman was there who had been crippled by a spirit for eighteen years. She was bent over and could not straighten up at all. When Jesus saw her, he called her forward and said to her, "Woman, you are set free from your infirmity." Then he put his hands on her, and immediately she straightened up and praised God.

Luke 13:11–13

Jews forbid work on the Sabbath

The generative acts of labor [prohibited on the Sabbath] are forty less one: he who sews, ploughs, reaps, binds sheaves, threshes, winnows, selects, grinds, sifts, kneads, bakes; he who shears wool, washes it, beats it, dyes it; spins, weaves, makes two loops, waves two threads, separates two threads; ties, unties, sews two stitches, tears in order to sew two stitches; he who traps a deer, slaughters it, flays it, salts it, cures its hide, scrapes it, and cuts it up; he who writes two letters, erases two letters in order to write two letters; he who builds, tears down; he who puts out a fire, kindles a fire; he who hits with a hammer; he who transports an object from one domain to another.

Mishnah *Shabbat* 7:2

Jews took the Sabbath seriously

Indignant because Jesus had healed on the Sabbath, the synagogue ruler said to the people, "There are six days for work. So come and be healed on those days, not on the Sabbath."

Luke 13:14

Tension between Jesus and
the synagogue leader

Opposite theologies

> The Lord answered him, "You hypocrites! Doesn't each of you on the
> Sabbath untie his ox or donkey from the stall and lead it out to give it water?
> Then should not this woman, a daughter of Abraham, whom Satan has kept
> bound for eighteen long years, be set free on the Sabbath day from what
> bound her?"
>
> Luke 13:15–16

Other Sabbath conflicts in Luke's gospel

Jesus is teaching Israel

David

One Sabbath Jesus was going through the grainfields, and his disciples began to pick some heads of grain, rub them in their hands and eat the kernels. Some of the Pharisees asked, "Why are you doing what is unlawful on the Sabbath?" Jesus answered them, "Have you never read what David did when he and his companions were hungry? He entered the house of God, and taking the consecrated bread, he ate what is lawful only for priests to eat. And he also gave some to his companions." Then Jesus said to them, "The Son of Man is Lord of the Sabbath."

Luke 6:1–5

Leper cleansed on a Sabbath

> On another Sabbath he went into the synagogue and was teaching, and a man was there whose right hand was shriveled. The Pharisees and the teachers of the law were looking for a reason to accuse Jesus, so they watched him closely to see if he would heal on the Sabbath. But Jesus knew what they were thinking and said to the man with the shriveled hand, "Get up and stand in front of everyone." So he got up and stood there. Then Jesus said to them, "I ask you, which is lawful on the Sabbath: to do good or to do evil, to save life or to destroy it?" He looked around at them all, and then said to the man, "Stretch out your hand." He did so, and his hand was completely restored. But they were furious and began to discuss with one another what they might do to Jesus.
>
> Luke 6:6–11

Jesus is Lord of the Sabbath

God can be honored on the Sabbath

> The synagogue ruler has more regard for the thirst of an animal over *one* Sabbath day, than for the Satan-bound condition of this woman over *eighteen years.*
>
> John Nolland

God works through Jesus

Jesus has come to forgive

A deeper reality in the healing

VIDEO DISCUSSION #1: MAKING DEEPER CONNECTIONS TO THE BIBLE

1. Why do you think the Jewish people in Jesus' time did not want him to heal on the Sabbath? (Be sure to talk about the reading from the Mishnah, see page 110).

2. Why do you think that Jesus did this healing on the Sabbath day, when he could have waited until the next day in order to avoid conflict with the Jewish leaders? What was he trying to teach the Jewish people by doing so?

3. The woman who was healed immediately praised God (Luke 13:13). Do you think that this was the correct response? Do you think she understood who Jesus was when he healed her? Why or why not?

4. Jesus' miracles always have a deeper meaning behind them. What do you think is the deeper meaning of this particular miracle?

CONNECTING THE BIBLE TO LIFE

Those who experience Jesus' restoring forgiveness are empowered to forgive others as well.

Video Teaching #2 Notes

Miracles are pictures of deeper realities

Jesus forgives us and sets us free

Although her prayers were unanswered for eighteen years, she was still faithful in synagogue worship.

IVP Women's Bible Commentary

The time: the kingdom of God overcomes Satan

> But if I drive out demons by the finger of God, then the kingdom of God has come to you.
>
> Luke 11:20

Jesus' authority

God's heart of restoration

Daughters and sons

> You are all sons of God through faith in Christ Jesus.
>
> Galatians 3:26

Jesus addresses her as "daughter of Abraham," thereby giving her value as a person of worth and dignity in the kingdom of God.

IVP Women's Bible Commentary

Socially restored

A new way of life: freedom

> Whether the challenge is being "bent over" and "brought low"
> by alcohol, drugs, sex, or some other debilitating situation, Jesus'
> deliverance is designed to free us up to relate to him in a way that
> enables us to shed the limitations Satan sometimes chains us with.
>
> Darrell Bock

Forgiving others

Models of forgiveness:

Corrie ten Boom

Jesus

VIDEO DISCUSSION #2: CONNECTING THE BIBLE TO LIFE

1. When Jesus forgives us, he also sets us free. How have you been set free by Jesus' forgiveness?

2. Darrell Bock says that this passage "beckons us to get right with God." Because God is a God of restoration, he desires to set us free. Are you "right with God"? Spend some time asking the Lord's forgiveness for anything that comes to mind.

3. Do you think that most Christians in your community are known as forgivers or grudge-bearers? What difference would it make if the entire Christian community in your city became forgivers? What differences would you see in your churches? What differences would you see in Christians themselves? What difference would you see in you?

4. When we are forgiven and set free, it is not to selfishness, but to serve others and to forgive others. Forgiving others not only helps them to move forward, but it helps *us* to move forward as well. Corrie ten Boom saw that those who were best able to forgive the atrocities that they experienced in the Holocaust were best able to rebuild their lives after the war. Think of a time when someone forgave you. How did it help you to "move forward"? Think of a time when you forgave someone. How did it help you to "move forward"?

MAKING DEEPER CONNECTIONS IN YOUR OWN LIFE

Personal reflection studies to do on your own.

Day One

1. Read Luke 7:11–17.

2. According to Luke 13:10–12, when Jesus saw the crippled woman in the synagogue, he called her forward. This raises two questions. First, are we too busy to "see" other people's needs? Is your schedule so full that you are running from one event to the next, with no time to stop and "see" other people's needs?

3. Second, this crippled woman was marginalized by those around her, who probably would have considered her as sinful. Do you, like Jesus, "see" the socially marginalized people in your world? Do you take time to help those whom most people ignore—not only those in your community but in your church? Think about people who need help in your church and community and what you might do to help them.

Day Two

1. Read Luke 7:36–50.

2. The synagogue ruler in Luke 13 was referring to the Sabbath commandment from Deuteronomy 5:12–14, "Observe the Sabbath day by keeping it holy, as the LORD your God has commanded you. Six days you shall labor and do all your work, but the seventh day is a Sabbath to the LORD your God." Jesus' reply refers to the animals cited in the rest of verse 14, "On it you shall not do any work, neither you, nor your son or daughter, nor your manservant or maidservant, nor your *ox*, your *donkey* or any of your animals." Not only did he know the Scriptures, but he knew the proper interpretation of them! Do you know Scripture well enough that if someone quoted a verse to you, you could cite the following verse? If you don't currently have a Bible memorization plan, consider starting one.

3. The woman who was healed in Luke 13 "praised God" (verse 13); the crowd was "delighted" (verse 17); the synagogue ruler was "indignant" and "humiliated" (verses 14, 17). Why do you think people reacted so differently? How do you react to God's compassion on others, especially those you might consider "unworthy" of it?

Day Three

1. Read Luke 8:40–53.

2. Let's not forget that the main point of the Luke 13 passage is that Jesus has come to bring forgiveness and loosen the bonds of Satan. As you pray today, thank God that he is a God of compassion who sent Jesus to secure your forgiveness by overpowering the evil one.

3. What does Luke 13 teach us about the coming of the kingdom of God? At the very least it shows us that Jesus is bringing the kingdom, where sickness is healed, Satan is overthrown, and the people rejoice. Have you seen these three elements of the kingdom in your life? If so, how?

Day Four

1. Read Luke 9:37–45.

2. Jesus asked, "Then should not this woman, a daughter of Abraham, whom Satan has kept bound for eighteen long years, be set free on the Sabbath day from what bound her?" (Luke 13:16). How does Satan "bind" people today? How do we, as ambassadors of the kingdom, help to set them free? Are you involved in ministries that set people free? Should you be involved in such ministries?

3. As you pray today, ask the Lord if you are forgiving others with the same willingness and grace with which he forgives you. Are there people whom you still have not forgiven?

Day Five

1. Read Luke 13:10–17 one more time.

2. Pray through the entire passage verse by verse, allowing the deeper meaning that you have discovered to lead you as you pray. Ask the Spirit to continue to remind you of what you have learned and to help you apply these truths to your life. Jot down any further applications that come to mind as you pray.

3. Turn back to the discussion questions from the video teaching (Video Discussion #1, #2). If there are questions that your group did not have time to discuss or questions that you might like to think more about, use this time to review and reflect further.

Source Acknowledgments

(These are noted in order of appearance for each session. Full source information can be found in "Books for Further Reading," beginning on page 129.)

Session 1

Page 11: Bock, *Luke*, NIVAC, 414.
Page 14: Bailey, *The Cross and the Prodigal*, InterVarsity Press, 2005, 29.
Page 16: Evans, *Luke*, 232.
Page 17: Bailey, *The Cross and the Prodigal*, 67.
Page 18: Ibid., 52.
Page 19: Nolland, *Luke*, 790.
Page 22: Morris, *Luke*, 260.
Page 23: Bock, *Luke*, NIVAC, 581.
Page 23: Ibid., 413.

Session 2

Page 31: Garland, *Mark*, 100.
Page 33: Bock, *Luke*, NIVAC, 162.
Page 34: Keener, *IVP Bible Background*, 139.
Page 35: Carson, *Matthew*, 205.
Page 35: France, *Mark*, 166.
Page 36: Ibid., 126.
Page 37: Garland, *Mark*, 97.
Page 41: In David Kinnaman, *Unchristian*, Baker, 2007, 181.
Page 42: Davies and Allison, *Matthew*, 93.

Session 3

Page 51: Köstenberger, in Beale and Carson, *Commentary on New Testament Use of Old Testament*, 460.

Page 53: Wilkins, *Matthew*, NIVAC, 372.
Page 54: Morris, *Matthew*, 428.
Page 54: Burge, *John*, 273.
Page 56: Wilkins, *Matthew*, NIVAC, 374.
Page 57: Burge, *John*, 276.
Page 60: Ibid., 280.
Page 62: Carson, *John*, 373.
Page 63: Burge, *John*, 271.

Session 4

Page 73: Garland, *Mark*, 20.
Page 76: Ibid., 18.
Page 77: Cole, *Mark*, 123.
Page 78: Morris, *Matthew*, 221.
Page 79: Strauss, *Luke*, 56.
Page 82: Guelich, *Mark*, 101.
Page 82: Garland, *Mark*, 104.
Page 83: Bock, *Luke*, NIVAC, 160.

Session 5

Page 89: Burge, *John*, 596.
Page 92: Köstenberger, *John*, BECNT, 590.
Page 93: Burge, *John*, 596.
Page 95: Köstenberger, *John*, BECNT, 596.
Page 98: Burge, *John*, 596.
Page 99: Osborne, *John*, 301.
Page 100: Burge, *John*, 598.

Session 6

Page 107: Bock, *Luke*, 1214.
Page 108: ten Boom, *Tramp for the Lord,* Berkley, 1978, 55.
Page 109: Strauss, *Luke*, 119.
Page 111: Green, *Luke*, 523.
Page 113: Nolland, *Luke*, 725.
Page 116: Kroeger and Evans, *IVP Women's Bible Commentary*, 577.
Page 118: Ibid.
Page 119: Bock, *Luke*, NIVAC, 376.

Map and Photo Credits

Maps: Courtesy of International Mapping

Jace Doron: page 90 (top)

T. J. Rathbun: pages 36, 52, 54, 55, 61, 62, 94, 111

Andy Sheneman: pages 11, 31, 51, 73, 89, 107

Jay King: page 75

Gordon Franz: page 93

Jane Haradine: page 112

istockphoto.com: pages 13, 14, 15, 17, 18, 19, 22, 23, 24, 33, 34, 35, 38, 40, 42, 53, 57, 60, 64, 76, 78, 79, 81, 82, 90 (bottom), 92, 95, 96, 98, 100, 101, 108, 109, 114, 116, 117, 118

Books for Further Reading

Life and Forgiveness of Jesus

Bailey, Kenneth E. *Jesus through Middle Eastern Eyes: Cultural Studies in the Gospels*. Downers Grove, Ill: InterVarsity Press, 2008.

Blomberg, Craig L. *Jesus and the Gospels: An Introduction and Survey*. Nashville: Broadman and Holman, 1997.

Bock, Darrell L. *Jesus According to Scripture: Restoring the Portrait from the Gospels*. Grand Rapids, Mich.: Baker, 2002.

Jones, L. Gregory. *Embodying Forgiveness: A Theological Analysis*. Grand Rapids, Mich.: Eerdmans, 1995.

Kraft, Charles H. *Deep Wounds Deep Healing: An Introduction to Deep Level Healing*. Ventura, Calif.: Regal, 2009.

Stein, Robert H. *Jesus the Messiah: A Survey of the Life of Christ*. Downers Grove, Ill.: InterVarsity Press, 1996.

Strauss, Mark L. *Four Portraits, One Jesus: An Introduction to Jesus and the Gospels*. Grand Rapids, Mich.: Zondervan, 2007.

Volf, Miroslav. *Free of Charge: Giving and Forgiving in a Culture Stripped of Grace*. Grand Rapids, Mich.: Zondervan, 2006.

Walker, Peter. *In the Steps of Jesus: An Illustrated Guide to the Places of the Holy Land*. Grand Rapids, Mich.: Zondervan, 2006.

Worthington, Everett L. *Forgiving and Reconciling: Bridges to Wholeness and Hope*. Downers Grove, Ill.: InterVarsity Press, 2003.

Four Gospels

Beale, G. K. and D. A. Carson, *Commentary on the New Testament Use of the Old Testament*. Grand Rapids, Mich.: Baker, 2007.

Evans, Craig A., gen. ed. *The Bible Knowledge Background Commentary: Matthew–Luke*. Colorado Springs: Victor Books, 2003.

Keener, Craig S. *The IVP Bible Background Commentary: New Testament*. Downers Grove, Ill.: InterVarsity Press, 1993.

Kroeger, Catherine Clark and Mary J. Evans, eds. *The IVP Women's Bible Commentary*. Downers Grove, Ill.: InterVarsity Press, 2002.

Matthew

Barton, Bruce B. *Matthew*. Life Application Bible Commentary. Wheaton, Ill.: Tyndale, 1996.

Blomberg, Craig L. *Matthew*. New American Commentary, vol. 22. Nashville: Broadman, 1992.

Carson, D. A. *Matthew, Mark, Luke*. The Expositor's Bible Commentary, vol. 8. Grand Rapids, Mich.: Zondervan, 1984.

Davies, W. D., Dale C. Allison Jr. *A Critical and Exegetical Commentary on the Gospel According to Saint Matthew*. The International Critical Commentary, 3 vols. Edinburgh: T&T Clark, 1988, 1991, 1997.

France, R. T. *The Gospel According to Matthew: An Introduction and Commentary*. Tyndale New Testament commentaries, vol. 1. Grand Rapids, Mich.: Eerdmans, 1985.

_____. *The Gospel of Matthew*. The New International Commentary on the New Testament. Grand Rapids, Mich.: Eerdmans, 2007.

Green, Michael. *The Message of Matthew: The Kingdom of Heaven*. The Bible Speaks Today Series. Downers Grove, Ill.: InterVarsity Press, 2000.

Guelich, Robert A. *Sermon on the Mount: A Foundation for Understanding*. Waco, Tex.: Word, 1982.

Gundry, Robert. *Matthew: A Commentary on His Handbook for a Mixed Church Under Persecution*. Grand Rapids, Mich.: Eerdmans, 2nd ed., 1994.

Hagner, Donald. *Matthew*. Word Biblical Commentary, vol. 33 a&b. Waco, Tex.: Word, 1993, 1995.

Keener, Craig S. *A Commentary on the Gospel of Matthew*. Grand Rapids, Mich.: Eerdmans, 1999.

Morris, Leon. *The Gospel According to Matthew*. The Pillar New Testament Commentary. Grand Rapids, Mich.: Eerdmans, 1992.

Mounce, Robert H. *Matthew*. New International Biblical Commentary, vol. 1. Peabody, Mass.: Hendrickson, 1991.

Nolland, John. *The Gospel of Matthew: A Commentary on the Greek Text*. The New International Greek Testament Commentary. Grand Rapids, Mich.: Eerdmans, 2005.

Simonetti, Manlio, ed. *Matthew*. Ancient Christian Commentary on Scripture. 2 vols. Downers Grove, Ill.: InterVarsity Press, 2002.

Turner, David L. *Matthew*. Baker Exegetical Commentary on the New Testament. Grand Rapids, Mich.: Baker, 2008.

Turner, David L. and Darrell L. Bock. *The Gospel of Matthew/The Gospel of Mark.* Cornerstone Biblical Commentary. Wheaton, Ill.: Tyndale, 2006.

Wilkins, Michael J. *Matthew: From Biblical Text to Contemporary Life.* The NIV Application Commentary. Grand Rapids, Mich.: Zondervan, 2004.

————. *Zondervan Illustrated Bible Backgrounds Commentary.* Grand Rapids, Mich.: Zondervan, 2002.

Mark

Cole, R. Alan. *The Gospel According to Mark.* Tyndale New Testament Commentaries, vol. 2. Grand Rapids, Mich.: Eerdmans, 2002.

Cranfield, C. E. B. *The Gospel According to Saint Mark: An Introduction and Commentary.* Cambridge Greek Testament Commentary. Cambridge University Press, 1972.

Edwards, James R. *The Gospel According to Mark.* The Pillar New Testament Commentary. Grand Rapids, Mich.: Eerdmans, 2002.

Evans, Craig. *Mark.* Word Biblical Commentary, vol. 34b. Nashville: Thomas Nelson, 2001.

Fackler, Mark. *Mark.* Life Application Bible Commentary. Wheaton, Ill.: Tyndale, 1994.

France, R. T. *The Gospel of Mark: A Commentary on the Greek Text.* The New International Greek New Testament Commentary. Grand Rapids, Mich.: Eerdmans, 2002.

Garland, David E. *Mark.* The NIV Application Commentary. Grand Rapids, Mich.: Zondervan, 1996.

————. *Zondervan Illustrated Bible Backgrounds Commentary.* Grand Rapids, Mich.: Zondervan, 2002.

Guelich, Robert A. *Mark.* Word Biblical Commentary, vol. 34a. Dallas: Word, 1989.

Gundry, Robert H. *A Commentary on His Apology for the Cross.* Grand Rapids, Mich.: Eerdmans, 1993.

Lane, William L. *The Gospel According to Mark: The English Text with Introduction, Exposition, and Notes.* The New International Commentary on the New Testament. Grand Rapids, Mich.: Eerdmans, 1974.

McKenna, David L. *Mark.* The Communicator's Commentary Series, vol. 2. Dallas: Word, 1982.

Oden, Thomas C. and Christopher A. Hall, eds. *Mark.* Ancient Christian Commentary on Scripture, vol. 2. Downers Grove, Ill.: InterVarsity Press, 1998.

Stein, Robert H. *Mark.* Baker Exegetical Commentary on the New Testament. Grand Rapids, Mich.: Baker, 2008.

Taylor, Vincent. *The Gospel According to St. Mark: The Greek Text with Introduction, Notes, and Indexes.* Thornapple Commentaries. Grand Rapids, Mich.: Baker, 2nd ed., 1981.

Wessel, Walter W. *Matthew, Mark, Luke.* The Expositor's Bible Commentary, vol. 8. Grand Rapids, Mich.: Zondervan, 1984.

Witherington, Ben III. *The Gospel of Mark: A Socio-Rhetorical Commentary.* Grand Rapids, Mich.: Eerdmans, 2001.

Luke

Barton, Bruce B., Dave Veerman, and Linda K. Taylor. *Luke.* Life Application Bible Commentary. Wheaton, Ill.: Tyndale, 1997.

Bock, Darrell L. *Luke.* The NIV Application Commentary. Grand Rapids, Mich.: Zondervan, 1996.

———. *Luke 1:1–9:50; 9:51–24:53.* Baker Exegetical Commentary on the New Testament, 2 vols. Grand Rapids, Mich.: Baker, 1996.

Evans, Craig A. *Luke.* New International Biblical Commentary, vol. 3. Peabody, Mass.: Hendrickson, 1990.

Fitzmyer, J. A. *The Gospel According to Luke : Introduction, Translation, and Notes.* Anchor Bible, vol. 28–28a. Garden City, N.Y.: Doubleday, 1981–1985.

Green, Joel B. *The Gospel of Luke.* New International Commentary on the New Testament. Grand Rapids, Mich.: Eerdmans, 1997.

Just, Arther A. Jr., ed. *Luke.* Ancient Christian Commentary on Scripture, vol. 3. Downers Grove, Ill.: InterVarsity Press, 2003.

Larson, Bruce. *Luke.* The Preacher's Commentary, vol. 26. Nashville: Thomas Nelson, 1983.

Liefeld, Walter L. *Matthew, Mark, Luke.* The Expositor's Bible Commentary, vol. 8. Grand Rapids, Mich.: Zondervan, 1984.

Marshall, I. Howard. *Luke: Historian and Theologian.* Grand Rapids, Mich.: Zondervan, 1980.

Morris, Leon. *Luke, An Introduction and Commentary.* Tyndale New Testament Commentaries, vol. 3. Grand Rapids, Mich.: Eerdmans, 1988.

Nolland, John. *Luke.* Word Biblical Commentary, vol. 35a–c. Dallas: Word, 1989–1993.

Stein, Robert H. *Luke.* The New American Commentary, vol. 24. Nashville: Broadman, 1992.

Strauss, Mark L. *Luke.* Zondervan Illustrated Bible Backgrounds Commentary. Grand Rapids, Mich.: Zondervan, 2002.

John

Barrett, C. K. *The Gospel According to St. John: An Introduction with Commentary and Notes on the Greek Text*. Philadelphia: Westminster Press, 1978.

Barton, Bruce B. *John*. Life Application Bible Commentary. Wheaton, Ill.: Tyndale, 1993.

Beasley-Murray, George R. *John*. Word Biblical Commentaries, vol. 36. Nashville: Thomas Nelson, 1999.

Brown, Raymond Edward. *The Gospel According to John*. Anchor Bible, vol. 29–29a. Garden City, N.Y., Doubleday, 1966–1970.

Burge, Gary M. *John*. The NIV Application Commentary. Grand Rapids, Mich.: Zondervan, 2000.

Card, Michael. *The Parable of Joy: Reflections on the Wisdom of the Book of John*. Nashville: Thomas Nelson, 1995.

Carson, Donald A. *The Gospel According to John*. The Pillar New Testament Commentary. Grand Rapids, Mich.: Eerdmans, 1991.

Keener, Craig S. *The Gospel of John: A Commentary*. 2 vols. Peabody, Mass.: Hendrickson, 2003.

Köstenberger, Andreas J. *John*. Baker Exegetical Commentary on the New Testament. Grand Rapids, Mich.: Baker, 2004.

_____. *Zondervan Illustrated Bible Backgrounds Commentary*. Grand Rapids, Mich.: Zondervan, 2002.

Morris, Leon. *The Gospel According to John*. New International Commentary on the New Testament. Grand Rapids, Mich.: Eerdmans, 1995.

Osborne, Grant R. *The Gospel of John*. Cornerstone Biblical Commentary, vol. 13. Carol Stream, Ill.: Tyndale, 2007.

Tasker, R. V. G. *The Gospel According to St. John: An Introduction and Commentary*. Tyndale New Testament Commentaries. Grand Rapids, Mich.: Eerdmans, 1960.

Tenney, Merrill C. *John, Acts*. The Expositor's Bible Commentary, vol. 9. Grand Rapids, Mich.: Zondervan, 1984.

Whitacre, Rodney A. *John*. The IVP New Testament Commentary Series, vol. 4. Downers Grove, Ill.: InterVarsity Press, 1999.

.

CHRISTIAN HISTORY MADE EASY

12-Session DVD Study for Individual or Group Use
by Timothy Paul Jones, PhD

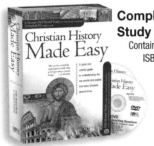

Complete *Christian History Made Easy* Study Kit
Contains each of the following items
ISBN: 9781596365254

The DVD
• All 12 DVD sessions, each about 30 minutes • Leader Guide on disc as a printable PDF • Fliers, bulletin inserts, posters & banners as PDFs on disc.
ISBN: 9781596365261

Leader Guide
• Leader Guide gives step-by-step instructions for group hosts or facilitators so you don't have to be the expert.
ISBN: 9781596365278

Participant Guide
• Purchase one for each participant.
• Includes group discussion questions, session outlines, key terms and definitions, Bible study questions, and more.
ISBN: 9781596365285

PowerPoint® Presentation
• Contains more than 300 slides to expand the scope of the teaching ISBN: 9781596363410

Christian History Made Easy Book
• 224 pages, paperback
ISBN: 9781596363281

www.ChristianHistoryMadeEasy.com

HOW WE GOT THE BIBLE

DVD Bible Study for Individual or Group Use

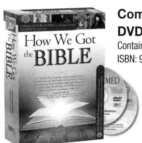

Complete *How We Got the Bible* DVD Bible Study Kit

Contains each of the following items
ISBN: 9781628622072

How We Got the Bible DVD Bible Study

• All six DVD sessions • Leader Guide on disc as a printable PDF •
Fliers, bulletin inserts, posters & banners as PDFs on disc
ISBN: 9781628622065

Leader Guide

• Leader Guide gives step-by-step instructions for group hosts or facilitators so you don't have to be the expert.
ISBN: 9781628622089

Participant Guide

• Purchase one for each participant.
• Includes group discussion questions, session outlines, key terms and definitions, Bible study questions, and more.
ISBN: 9781628622126

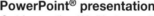

PowerPoint® presentation

• Contains more than 100 slides to expand the scope of the teaching ISBN: 9781890947460

Pamphlet

• Fold-out time line of key events
ISBN: 9781628620825

How We Got the Bible handbook

• Goes into more depth
• Explores the historical background
• 180-page paperback
ISBN: 9781628622164

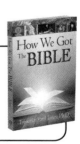

www.HowWeGotTheBibleDVD.com

FEASTS OF THE BIBLE

DVD Bible Study for Individual or Group Use

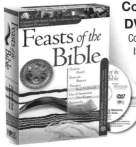

Complete *Feasts of the Bible* DVD Bible Study Kit
Contains each of the following items
ISBN: 9781596364646

Feasts of the Bible DVD Bible Study Leader Pack
• All six DVD-based sessions • Leader Guide on disc as a printable PDF • Fliers, bulletin inserts, posters & banners as PDFs on disc ISBN: 9781596364653

Leader Guide
• Leader Guide gives step-by-step instructions for group hosts or facilitators so you don't have to be the expert
ISBN: 9781596364660

Participant Guide
• Each participant will need a guide
• Guide contains definitions, charts, comparisons, Bible references, discussion questions, and more
ISBN: 9781596364677

Feasts of the Bible PowerPoint® presentation
• Contains more than 100 slides to expand the scope of the teaching ISBN: 9781596361775

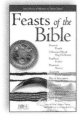

Feasts of the Bible pamphlet
• Chart showing each feast, the date, biblical passage, and symbolism fulfilled by Jesus
ISBN: 9781890947583

Messiah in the Feasts of Israel handbook
• Goes into greater depth on all the feasts
• Gives insights into God's redemptive plan, discusses the prophetic purposes of the feasts
• 236-page paperback
ISBN: 9780970261977

www.FeastsOfTheBible.com

We want to hear from you. Please send your comments about this book to us in care of info@hendricksonrose.com. Thank you.

www.hendricksonrose.com